6/27/14

IS NOTHING SOMETHING?

KIDS' QUESTIONS AND ZEN ANSWERS ABOUT LIFE, DEATH, FAMILY, FRIENDSHIP, AND EVERYTHING IN BETWEEN

THICH NHAT HANH

ILLUSTRATED BY JESSICA MCCLURE

PLUM BLOSSOM BOOKS
BERKELEY, CALIFORNIA

Plum Blossom Books is the children's imprint of Parallax Press.

© 2014 by Unified Buddhist Church
All rights reserved.
Printed in Malaysia

Edited by Rachel Neumann
Illustrated by Jessica McClure / jessicamccluredesigns.com
Cover and interior design by Debbie Berne

Library of Congress Cataloging-in-Publication Data
is available upon request.

1 2 3 4 5 / 18 17 16 15 14

A good question doesn't need to be long. If it comes from your heart, it can help a lot of people.

These questions are real questions that real children have asked me. I always try to give an answer that offers the best of myself. I am much older than the children who asked these questions, but when we sit and breathe together, it seems that we are the same. We are each other's continuation.

THICH NHAT HANH

Why does the world exist?
6

Is nothing something?
7

What does God look like?
8

How long am I going to live?
9

Why is the sun so hot?
10

What is mindfulness?
11

Why are there good days and why are there bad days?
12

Why do we have to recycle things? Can't we just throw them away?
14

Why do people make wars?
15

I love my grandfather but he died. How can he still be with me?
16

How can I remain calm when I see so many bad things in the world?
17

How can I love someone who likes different things than me?
18

Why do I sometimes feel lonely and that no one loves me?
19

How can I control my temper?
20

What do you do when you're scared?
22

How can I stop worrying so much?
23

What should I do when I feel sad?
24

What should you do if someone feels bad and you want to comfort that person and make him or her feel better?
25

Why do kids watch TV?
26

How do you know if somebody is a real friend?
30

When my parents divorced, they fought a lot. Why can't they live together?
27

Why is my brother always so nasty toward me?
28

I just moved to a new school. How do I make friends?
33

I'm having a problem with someone, but I'm too shy to speak to this person. What do I do?
31

Why do I sometimes feel that everyone is against me?
32

Why don't monks and nuns eat meat?
37

What is meditation and why do people do it?
35

Why do people sometimes listen to a bell when they meditate?
36

Mindful Breathing
46

Who was the Buddha?
39

Who is Thich Nhat Hanh?
40

May I give you a hug?
45

Mindful Walking
47

Why does the world exist?

Nobody knows why the world exists, but we can still appreciate it. There are so many wonderful things in the world. Your body is a wonder. The flower is a wonder. The stars are wonders. If you only notice the unpleasant things, that's a pity. Even the things that don't look beautiful at first are wonders. A lotus flower grows in mud. If there were no mud, there would be no lotus. So the lotus flower is a wonder and the mud is also a wonder. When you are aware of the wonders around you, life is full of joy.

Is nothing something?

Yes. Nothing is something. You have an idea in your head of nothing. You have an idea in your head of something. Both are things that can create either suffering or happiness.

What does God look like?

God expresses him- or herself in many ways. We can see God in a flower, in the sun, in a river, and in our friend. God doesn't have a particular form; God is always expressed in the beauty of the here and the now.

How long am I going to live?

Here is some good news. If you look deeply into everything, you can see that you will live forever. You will never die; you'll just change form. You are like a cloud. A cloud can become snow or rain, but it can't die. You are like a wave in the ocean. After you rise and fall as a wave, you will still be part of the ocean. Your shape will change but you won't disappear.

Why is the sun so hot?

Every single thing has its own nature, the way it's supposed to be. If the sun wasn't hot enough, living things wouldn't be warm enough and we would die. We need the sun to be hot just like we need the tree to be green and we need people to be gentle. Children can practice being kind and gentle by walking and breathing mindfully. Then they are doing their part and the sun is doing its part and we are helpful to each other.

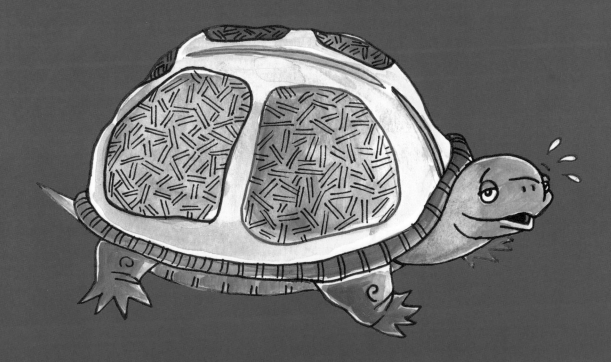

What is mindfulness?

Mindfulness is energy. This energy helps us enjoy what is happening right now. Mindful energy can bring us a lot of joy. It helps us suffer less and learn from our suffering. A good way to get some mindful energy is to close your eyes and breathe easily. Just pay attention to your breath. If you can enjoy your in-breath and out-breath, you are creating mindful energy.

Why are there good days and why are there bad days?

We say, "Have a good day," to people because we want them to enjoy being alive that day. But sometimes things happen that we can't help. We may break or damage something. Someone may be mean or unfriendly to us. When these things happen, it's easy to forget to be aware of our breathing.

We forget how good it feels to walk on the Earth. Our minds can get stuck on the bad thing that happened and what is going wrong, and we forget what is good and what is going right.

It helps to remember our mindful walking and mindful breathing. Our mindfulness is like magic that turns a bad day into a good one. When we remember to breathe and walk mindfully, it feels so good that our bad feelings just dissolve.

There is a way to start the day and make sure it will be a good one right from the beginning. Before leaving home in the morning, you and your family can sit down together. If you have a bell, all of you can listen to the bell calmly. Then you can practice mindful breathing and say to yourself: "Breathing in, I calm myself; breathing out, I smile." If you start the day like this, your day will go better.

Why do we have to recycle things? Can't we just throw them away?

We don't want this beautiful planet to become a mess. We have to preserve the beauty and freshness of this planet so that the children who will be born later will also be able to enjoy it and not be surrounded by garbage and by air that is hard to breathe.

Your anger and jealousy are also like garbage. With mindfulness, we can recycle these strong feelings and transform them back into friendship.

Why do people make wars?

People fight each other because they have anger, fear, and craving inside themselves. They want more wealth and resources than they have, and they believe that they can get more of what they want by hurting others. Fear and anger are born from misunderstanding. If we want more peace in the world, we can start by taking care of the misunderstanding in ourselves.

I love my grandfather but he died. How can he still be with me?

If your loved one isn't there in his familiar form, look for him in his new forms. A kernel of corn grows into a corn stalk, and the stalk makes an ear of corn, which contains new kernels. Your grandfather is like the original corn kernel and you are the new corn kernel. In this way, you are his continuation. Your grandfather is still alive in every cell of your body. You can have as many conversations with him as you want.

How can I remain calm when I see so many bad things in the world?

Whenever I see violence or cruelty, it still makes me angry. We all get angry sometimes. But we can learn to take care of our anger. If we look closely, we can notice that people who are cruel have a lot of suffering inside. When we see this, we can be compassionate, and help the situation by creating peace, even if what is happening around us is not very peaceful. We can use our breath and our mindfulness to transform the energy of anger into the energy of compassion. When we have the energy of compassion, we can do a lot of things to help people suffer less.

How can I love someone who likes different things than me?

To love is to discover. If you keep on loving another person, you will keep discovering wonderful things about that person. You can enjoy the differences because it would be boring if everyone were the same. Even if the other person has a quality that doesn't seem lovable, you can practice loving that person anyway, just as they are, and not how you wish they were.

18

Why do I sometimes feel lonely and that no one loves me?

Sometimes the people around you are distracted and may forget to express their love. But if you feel like no one loves you, you can always look outside at the natural world. Do you see a tree out there? That tree loves you. It offers its beauty and freshness to you and gives you oxygen so you can breathe. The Earth loves you, offering you fresh water and delicious fruit for you to eat. The world expresses its love in many ways, not just with words.

How can I control my temper?

The very first thing we can do when we're angry is to *notice* we're angry. Sometimes we're angry, but we don't want to accept it. When I'm angry, I like to stop and become aware of my breath and say,

Breathing in, I know anger is in me.
Breathing out, I will take good care of my anger.

Once we're aware of our anger, we can be gentle with it. Don't try to control your anger. As soon as you try to control it, this may start a fight between you and your temper. Instead, just be with it and accept it. Once you've sat with your anger for a while, you will find that it doesn't need to explode. It will transform on its own, without hurting anyone.

What do you do when you're scared?

Usually, when we're afraid, we try to run away from whatever scares us. When I am scared, I breathe deeply and calm myself. I try to stop my thinking and just breathe. This always helps me. Every time I have an upset stomach, I fill a hot water bottle and I put it on my stomach. In five minutes I feel much better. My mindful breathing is like a hot water bottle for my mind. Every time I apply mindful breathing to my fear, I get relief.

How can I stop worrying so much?

When we worry, it's usually about something that has already happened or something that we think might happen in the future. But all we can take care of is the present moment. Suppose we are traveling and we know we will have to cross a bridge. We can't cross the bridge until we get there. If we spend our time thinking about how to cross the bridge, we'll miss out on the journey. If we stay in the present moment, then when we finally get to the bridge, we can cross without fear.

What should I do when I feel sad?

A wonderful thing to do is smile to your sadness. This is a very simple practice but it has a great effect. Your smile is like the sunshine. There can be sunshine with the rain. You can smile and cry at the same time and it will be like you are making a rainbow.

What should you do if someone feels bad and you want to comfort that person and make him or her feel better?

One of the simplest and most loving things you can do for someone who feels bad is just to be with them and breathe with them. You can say, "I am here for you." You are offering your presence, which is the most wonderful gift you can offer another person.

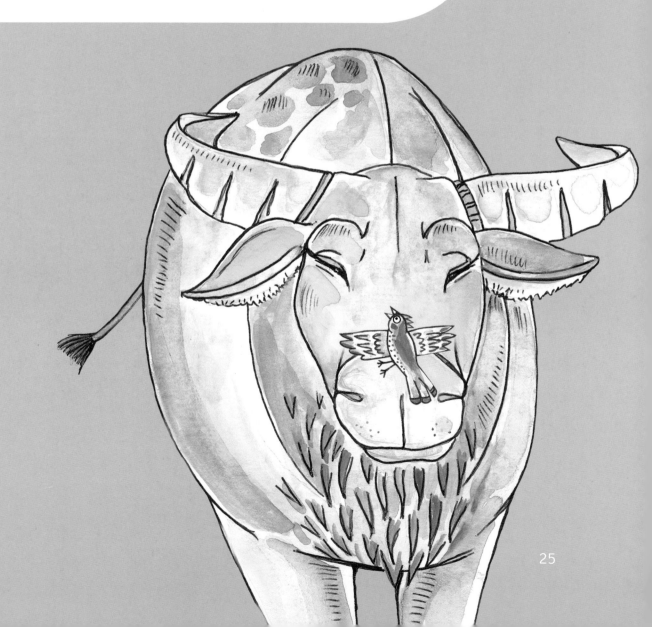

Why do kids watch TV?

Sometimes when the grown-ups who are taking care of the children are too busy, a television or a video game becomes a babysitter. But it is not usually a good caregiver. There are many messages of violence and greed on the screen that we absorb without realizing it. If we watch a screen a lot, we forget to enjoy all the beautiful things around us. If we save screen time for special occasions, we will enjoy those times more.

When my parents divorced, they fought a lot. Why can't they live together?

If our parents separate, it's not because they want to make us suffer but because they have difficulties that they can't overcome. Living together is not easy. If you are still a kid and you start practicing love and understanding now, it may be easier to live with other people when you grow up because you will have had a lot of practice with compassion.

Why is my brother always so nasty toward me?

Someone who is nasty is someone who is not very happy. When you are happy you are not mean to others.

Take a quiet moment and ask yourself, "Why is that person being mean? Why is that person unhappy?" You can also ask yourself if you are ever mean to your brother.

It can be a challenge to be patient with our brothers and sisters. We usually think the other person is wrong and we want them to change. But we are also partly responsible for their behavior. If we are more compassionate, more patient, more loving and more understanding, we can help our siblings change more quickly. In order to change our siblings, we have to change ourselves first.

How do you know if somebody is a real friend?

It takes time. In everyone there is a seed of loyalty and there is a seed of betrayal. If we strengthen our own loyalty and are loyal to our friends, we will encourage them to be loyal as well. So instead of worrying whether the other person will betray us one day, we can help that person to cultivate more loyalty and he or she will stay with us and be our friend for a long time.

I'm having a problem with someone, but I'm too shy to speak to this person. What do I do?

You can write down your question or your concern, and why it is bothering you, and you can give it to him or her in writing.

Why do I sometimes feel that everyone is against me?

Don't wait for other people to accept you. You can learn to accept and love yourself. When you do this, you will be more focused on giving your love to others and less focused on how others feel about you. People will see this and they will be more able to express their love and appreciation for you in turn.

I just moved to a new school. How do I make friends?

A new school can be very exciting. Don't worry. Just allow things to happen. New friends will come to you, if you are ready. When you go to the mountains for vacation, you will discover many beautiful trees and flowers and things that you have never seen before. You can't predict what you will see. A new school is like that.

What is meditation and why do people do it?

To meditate is to concentrate and look inward. You can sit down to meditate but you can also meditate while walking to school, lying in the grass, or resting in your bed at night. If you are quiet and enjoying your in-breath and out-breath, you're practicing meditation. If you know how to smile beautifully and without effort, then you know how to meditate. It's not difficult.

If I ask you why you eat ice cream, you would say, "Because I like it." Meditation is the same. I do it because I like it. To meditate is to have fun.

Why do people sometimes listen to a bell when they meditate?

The sound of the bell is the sound of a friend calling you back to the present moment. Any sound that reminds you to pay attention to your breathing is a bell of mindfulness. The school bell, the sound of a phone ringing, a clock chime, or a timer in the kitchen are all good bells of mindfulness.

Why don't monks and nuns eat meat?

We don't eat meat because we want to reduce the suffering of living beings. Human beings suffer, but animals also suffer. So eating vegetarian food is one of the ways to lessen the suffering of living beings. Knowing this, we don't suffer when we refrain from eating meat. In fact, we feel wonderful when we can follow a vegetarian diet because we feel that we can cultivate more compassion, more love. Even if you are not a monk or a nun, if you eat less meat it shows your concern and love for other living beings and for our planet.

Who was the Buddha?

There are many buddhas, but the buddha who is most well-known on Earth was a human being named Siddhartha who was born about 2,600 years ago in a small kingdom called Shakya, which is in present-day Nepal. Siddhartha was a prince. When he saw that the people around him suffered so much, he went to the forest and practiced for many years to figure out how to help people suffer less. After sitting in meditation for a long time, he became the Buddha, which means "the awakened one."

There is a buddha, a compassionate, awakened person, already inside each of us. Whenever we forgive someone, or love someone, or are compassionate and kind, we are already a buddha. Every living being can become a buddha, not just people, but birds, fish, deer, and every animal we know.

Where are you from?

I am from many places. I come from my father; I come from my mother; I come from my teacher; and I come from the air, from the clouds, and from the Earth. I have come from many places.

How old are you?

I am the continuation of the Buddha, so I am 2,600 years old.

I am also the continuation of my father, who would be over 100 years old today if he were still alive.

At the same time, I am a continuation of you, who asked the question, so I am also six years old.

How are you?

I am like this: calm enough and happy being in the here and now.

Where do you live and what do you do there?

I live in a community in the southwest of France called Plum Village. There are many monks and nuns there. There are also many people who aren't monks and nuns who stay and practice with us. We live together. We wake up at the same time in the morning and we practice mindful sitting, walking, cooking, eating, washing up, and working together all year round. We enjoy it very much.

From time to time, we go to another country to visit and teach so we have made a lot of friends all over the world. Our friends are our spiritual family, so we think of our family as being everywhere.

What's it like in Plum Village?

It's difficult to describe, so you should come visit. When someone who has never eaten an orange asks, "What does an orange taste like?" it's so difficult to describe. So please come and experience it for yourself.

Do you play sports?

I used to play soccer and ping-pong a lot and I still like to play ping-pong now and then. But most of all I like walking mindfully.

How do you give talks to so many people without getting nervous?

How do you know that I don't get nervous? I remember the first time I had to stand up and give a talk, I was scared. But with practice, I started to feel less nervous and my talks got better. So the answer is to keep practicing.

I was wondering if you like your job.

I do.

How did you choose to be a monk?

I have a seed of monkhood in me. When I was a little boy, I saw a drawing of the Buddha on the cover of a magazine. He was sitting very peacefully on the grass. This impressed me very much, because the people around me were very nervous and not calm and happy at all. That was the first time I wanted to become a monk. Being a monk is one of the ways to become a buddha. Being a monk, you don't need a big salary. You only need enough money to buy toothpaste, or to call your family, or to visit them from time to time. You don't need much money. So you don't need to work all that much. You devote a lot of your time to helping people who come to you so they can learn how to practice mindfulness. You take care of them and show them the way to sit, to walk, and to breathe mindfully. When you can help people so they suffer less, when you can make them smile, you feel great. You feel rewarded. But you can be a buddha even if you are not a monk. You can be a buddha in your regular life today.

Why do monks and nuns shave their heads?

There are many ways of answering that question. One way would be to say that we don't want to spend too much money on shampoo! Another answer is that we want to let people know we are already a monk or a nun so they should not try to make us their wife or their husband. Also, monks and nuns want to be reminded that they are monks and nuns. So when we look in the mirror or touch our heads, we are reminded that we don't have hair and we remember the vows we have made as monks and nuns.

Why do you bow to your meals?

I bow before I eat because I want to express my gratitude. There are so many who are hungry in the world. If I have the chance to have food to eat every day, I feel grateful.

Do you remember any of your past lives?

Yes. When I practice looking deeply, I see that at one time in the past I was a rock, a tree, a squirrel, a bird, a fish, a cloud, and a river. If I continue to look deeply, I see that I am still a rock, a cloud, a mountain, a river, and a squirrel; I continue to be them. I have been all these kinds of beings and so have you. We continue to be all of them. They are still in us. We inter-are with them.

You may think that you are only a human being. But if you look deeply, you can see that you are also a cloud. Drinking a cloud is what we do every day, but we don't realize it. The cloud becomes the rain; the rain becomes the water; and you drink a cloud in the form of tea, or water, or juice. With the practice of looking deeply, we can see our former lives. We continue to carry our former lives with us in the present moment.

Have you ever hurt someone on purpose?

I have hurt people through lack of mindfulness and through ignorance, but not with the intention of making the other person suffer. I don't want to make anyone suffer, but because I'm not always calm enough, or mindful enough, I have hurt others. I have done that a few times, and I always regret it. I vow to myself that I will be more careful and I will not do it again next time.

When did you start practicing peace?

I used to try to create peace, but I was not successful. Then, one day I realized that breathing in and breathing out mindfully could help bring peace to my body and mind. That was the day I truly started practicing peace.

May I give you a hug?

Mindful Breathing

Everyone can practice breathing mindfully. Just breathe slowly and gently and notice the air as it goes in and out of your body. Mindful breathing can help us enjoy the moment and notice when we are happy, healthy, loved, and safe. Mindful breathing can also help us calm and comfort ourselves when we are hurt, sad, frightened, or angry.

Put a finger under your nose and feel the air as it passes in and out of your nostrils. Try it right now! The air you breathe in is cool and fresh. The air you breathe out is moist and warm. Sit up straight, relax, and put your hands on your belly. Feel how it moves in and out, expanding when you breathe in and relaxing when you breathe out.

Try lying down on the floor and feeling your belly rise and fall. Place a toy animal, a flower, a feather, or a small paper boat on your belly and watch it ride the waves as you breathe in and out, allowing the air to go all the way down to your abdomen and out again.

If you really want to be good at mindful breathing, you have to practice regularly. You can practice anytime and anywhere: in a quiet spot at home, waiting for dinner, outside, in the car, or on the bus going to school, even in the classroom.

Here is one way to practice: Make sure you are comfortable and that you can breathe easily. You can close your eyes if you want to. Then just notice your breathing, in and out. Don't change it, just notice if it's long or short, deep or shallow, fast or slow. While you are following your breathing, you can imagine you are a fresh and beautiful flower, a strong and stable mountain, or a still, calm lake. Inside you there is a lot of space.

Mindful Walking

An elephant is so big and heavy and yet it walks gently and softly. A cat can leap quickly, but its body is relaxed and supple. Animals don't worry when they walk. They don't drag their feet. Imagine you have huge feet like a kind and gentle elephant, or the soft paws of a sleek cat, or the long legs of a proud ostrich, its head held high.

Begin by walking slowly. Don't get distracted with talking or thinking about things. Take one step and breathe in; take another step and breathe out. Relax and feel the contact of your feet with the Earth. Feel the soles of your feet as they touch the ground. Notice how your foot rolls from heel to toe and then lifts up. Feel your feet carrying all the weight of your body. Put all your weight on one foot and then on the other. Can you stop and lift up one foot mid-stride without losing balance, like a flamingo? Walk softly and gently, as if you are kissing the Earth with each step. By walking mindfully, you are thanking the Earth for giving you the food, air, water, and beauty you need to live.

We can practice walking mindfully anywhere. Walking down the street or walking to the bathroom, we can focus on breathing and walking calmly and not rushing. We can just enjoy walking and not rush to get anywhere. If we are outside, we may notice the tiny ants, the caterpillar, the slug, or the snail on our path. Don't step on them! They are our friends and companions. When we walk mindfully, we get to really enjoy being alive on this planet, wherever we are.

Plum Blossom Books, the children's imprint of Parallax Press, publishes books on mindfulness for young people, parents, and educators.

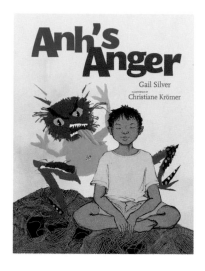

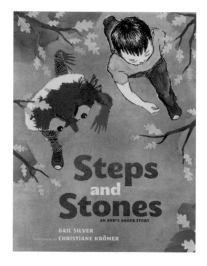

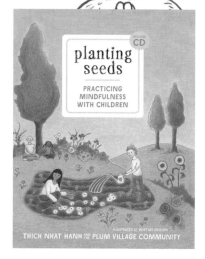

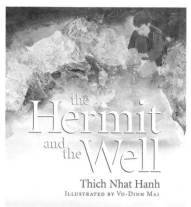

Parallax Press
P.O. Box 7355
Berkeley, California 94707

parallax.org